CONTENTS

WHAT'S THE WEATHER? 4

WIND 10

CLOUDS 14

RAIN, SNOW AND HAIL 18

WEATHER FORECASTS 26

CLIMATE 28

GLOSSARY 30

FURTHER INFORMATION 31

INDEX 32

WHAT'S THE WEATHER?

Take a look outside. What's the weather like? Is it sunny or is it raining? Perhaps there is snow on the ground. Whatever the weather is like today, you can be sure of one thing. It will be different tomorrow. It may be slightly cooler or slightly warmer. It might be cloudy, or raining. The weather will hardly ever be exactly the same.

HOW THE WEATHER AFFECTS US

Many of the things we do, what we wear and what we eat, are affected by the weather. When it is cold, we stay indoors or dress warmly if we have to go outside. We eat more hot meals and drink hot things to warm us up.

DISCOVERING GEOGRAPHY

WEATHER

Rebecca Hunter

www.raintreepublishers.co.uk

Visit our website to find out more information about **Raintree** books.

To order:
 Phone 44 (0) 1865 888112
 Send a fax to 44 (0) 1865 314091
 Visit the Raintree Bookshop at **www.raintreepublishers.co.uk** to browse our catalogue and order online.

First published in Great Britain by Raintree,
Halley Court, Jordan Hill, Oxford
OX2 8EJ, part of Harcourt Education.

Raintree is a registered trademark of Harcourt Education Ltd.

Produced for Raintree by Discovery Books Ltd
Design: Ian Winton
Editorial: Rebecca Hunter
Consultant: Jeremy Bloomfield
Commissioned photography: Chris Fairclough
Illustrations: Keith Williams, Stefan Chabluk and Pamela Goodchild
Production: Jonathan Smith

Originated by Dot Gradations Ltd
Printed and bound in China by South China Printing Company

ISBN 1 844 21682 9 (hardback)
07 06 05 04 03
10 9 8 7 6 5 4 3 2 1

ISBN 1 844 21687 X (paperback)
08 07 06 05 04
10 9 8 7 6 5 4 3 2 1

British Library Cataloguing in Publication Data
Hunter, Rebecca
Weather. – (Discovering Geography)
551.6
A full catalogue record for this book is available from the British Library.

Acknowledgements
The publishers would like to thank the following for permission to reproduce photographs:
Bruce Coleman pp. **5**, top **16**, **17** (Dr Scott Nielsen), **21** top, (Andrew Purcell), **21** bottom, **23** top (Konrad Wothe); Chris Fairclough p. **26**; Getty Images pp. **4** (Adamski Peek), **5** bottom (Timothy Shonnard), **6** (David Olsen), **7** top (Rob D. Casey), bottom (Karl Weatherly), **10** (Donovan Reese), **12** (Patrick Cocklin), **14** (Mike McQueen), **15** (Paul Chesley), **20** (Don Spiro), **22** (David Woodfall), **23** bottom, (Jeremy Walker), **24** (Eddie Soloway), **25** top (Cameron Davidson), bottom (Alan R. Moller), **29** top (Larry Ulrich), bottom (David Sutherland); Oxford Scientific Films p. **28** (Michael Fogden); Science Photo Library p. **27**.

Cover photograph of a thunderstorm reproduced with permission of Bruce Coleman (Gunter Ziesler).

The publishers would like to thank the following schools for their help in providing equipment, models and locations for photography sessions: Bedstone College, Bucknell, Moor Park, Ludlow and Packwood Haugh, Shrewsbury.

Every effort has been made to contact copyright holders of any material reproduced in this book.
Any omissions will be rectified in subsequent printings if notice is given to the publishers.

Any words appearing in the text in bold, **like this**, are explained in the Glossary.

In the summer when the days are long and sunny, we might go to the beach or swimming pool. We wear fewer clothes, and we like to eat ice cream and drink cold drinks.

▶ *In summer we usually wear less clothes than in winter – especially at the beach. It is very important to protect your skin with sun cream.*

▼ *It is fun playing outside in the rain – as long as you are dressed for it!*

What Makes Weather?

Things such as **temperature**, wind, rain, clouds and sunshine are all aspects of the weather.

World Weather

The weather is different all over the world. It is different from country to country and also varies within a country. In many parts of the world, the weather changes with the **seasons**. Summers are usually hot with brief showers or heavy thunderstorms. Winters are colder and may even be snowy.

A rainbow appears during showers in Hawaii, USA.

PREDICTING THE WEATHER

It would be nice to be able to tell what the weather will be like tomorrow. By learning what causes the weather and being able to understand some of its signs, we can try to **predict** what is going to happen.

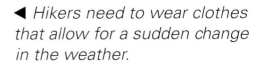

◀ Hikers need to wear clothes that allow for a sudden change in the weather.

THE ATMOSPHERE

Weather is caused by changes in the **atmosphere**.

The atmosphere is the name we give to the layer of gases around Earth. The atmosphere is about 1000 kilometres (620 miles) thick.

Nearly all clouds form in the bottom 10–12 kilometres (6–7 miles) of the atmosphere, and this is where most of the weather happens.

HEATING EARTH

Earth is heated by the Sun. Different parts of Earth receive different amounts of heat. Places along the **equator** are the hottest places because the Sun heats this area from directly overhead. The North and South Poles are the coldest places because Earth's surface is curved, so the Sun's rays are spread out over a wider area.

Sun

Sun's rays

North Pole

South Pole

THERMOMETERS

We can tell how hot or cold a place is by measuring the **temperature** of the air with a **thermometer**. A thermometer is a tube that contains a special liquid. This liquid rises up the tube as it is heated and falls as it cools. A scale is printed next to it. The scale is like the scale on a ruler but instead of measuring in centimetres, a thermometer measures in degrees Celsius (°C) or degrees Fahrenheit (°F).

PROJECT

What is the temperature where you live?

You will need:
a garden thermometer
a note pad.

1. Hang the thermometer in an open space in your garden, but make sure it is in the shade. The side of your house or the trunk of a tree would be a good place.

2. Measure the temperature at the same time every day. The day will probably be warmest at around 2 p.m. Try to take the temperature as close to this time as possible.

3. Write the results in your note pad.

4. Do this at different times of the year. Then you will be able to see the change in temperature from **season** to season.

WIND

Air that moves across Earth's surface is called wind – but what makes the air move?

When air is heated, it rises. You can see this happening when a hot-air balloon takes off. Gas burners heat the air inside the balloon. When the air is hot enough, the whole balloon is lifted off the ground into the sky.

MOVING AIR

A similar thing happens when the Sun heats the land. The warm land heats the air above it, and the warmed air starts to rise. In other parts of the **atmosphere**, air is cooling down. Cool air sinks down and moves in to take the place of the warm air rising in other places. This movement of air across the land is wind.

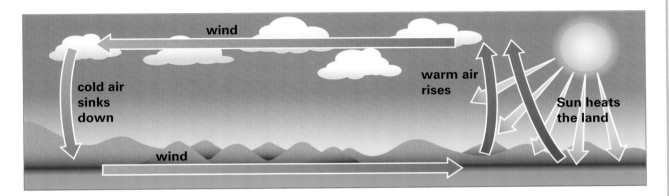

WORLD WINDS

This map shows some of the winds that blow across Earth. These global winds are called trade winds because ships carrying goods once relied on them to sail around the world.

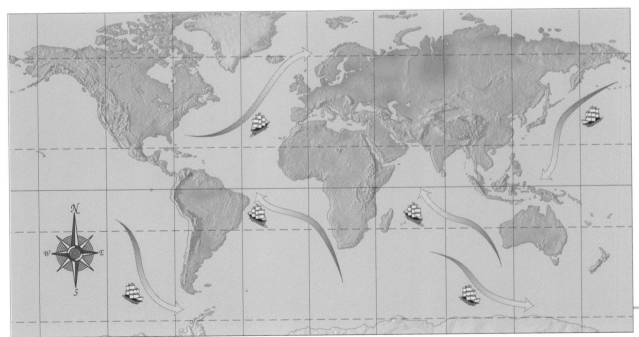

MEASURING THE WIND

We can record the wind in two ways. We can look at its direction and we can measure its speed.

WIND DIRECTION

We always record the direction a wind is coming from. A westerly wind is coming from the west, an easterly wind from the east, and so on. We record wind direction using a weather vane.

WIND SPEED

In 1805, Commander Francis Beaufort worked out a scale for measuring the effects of wind at different speeds. This scale is called the Beaufort scale. It measures the effects of wind from air that is barely moving (force 1) through to a full-scale **hurricane** (force 12). Wind speed is measured in kilometres or miles per hour with a device called an **anemometer**.

BEAUFORT SCALE

1. Smoke drifts gently.

2. Leaves rustle.

3. Leaves and twigs on trees move.

4. Flags flutter.

5. Small branches move.

6. Large branches move.

PROJECT

Make a weather vane.

You will need:
a drinking straw
a pin
a bead
a cork
a wooden garden stake
some coloured cardboard
scissors
sticky tape.

1. Make a short cut lengthways in each end of the straw.

2. Cut a pointed fish head and tail (or any other animal) out of the cardboard and push it into the ends of the straw.

3. Fix the cork with sticky tape to the garden stake.

4. Push the pin through the middle (balance point) of the straw, then through the bead and into the cork.

5. Push the stake into the ground in an open space.

6. Ask an adult to show you where north is, and mark an 'N' on the cork. Mark the positions of south, west and east in the same way.

7. Whole trees sway.

8. Branches break off trees.

9. Tiles blow off roofs.

10. Trees blown down.

11. Serious damage to property.

12. Hurricane – wind speed over 120 kmph.

CLOUDS

Clouds are a good way of telling what kind of weather to expect in the next few hours or days. A sky full of dark, thick clouds almost certainly means rain. Fluffy, white clouds that form on sunny days mean the weather will probably stay warm and dry.

WHAT ARE CLOUDS MADE OF?

This may sound strange, but clouds are made of water. Water can exist in three forms. We usually see it as a liquid in ponds and rivers or coming out of a tap. If we freeze it, it becomes a solid called ice. The third form of water is a gas called water vapour.

EVAPORATION AND CONDENSATION

Water vapour cannot be seen, but the air is always full of it. On a sunny day, a puddle of water will quickly dry up. The water has not really disappeared, it has turned into water vapour in the air. This process is called **evaporation**.

When water vapour cools down, it will turn back into tiny drops of liquid water. Water vapour turning into water again is called **condensation**. If you breathe on to a cold window, the water vapour in your breath condenses into tiny droplets of water on the window pane.

Water vapour from a kettle condenses on a cold window.

Water vapour evaporates from rivers, lakes and oceans all the time. Clouds form when warm air carrying this water vapour rises. Air rises when it is warmed by the land, or when the wind pushes it up and over hills.

As the air rises, it cools, and the water vapour condenses into tiny water droplets. These tiny droplets join together to make clouds. Each cloud is made of millions of tiny droplets of water.

TYPES OF CLOUD

There are three main types of cloud:

Stratus clouds form as sheets of low grey cloud that often cover the whole sky. They usually mean light rain or drizzle.

Cumulus clouds (below) mean fine weather. They look like puffs of cotton wool and are usually formed on sunny days.

Cirrus clouds are thin, wispy clouds that are very high up in the sky. At this level it is so cold that the clouds are not made of water droplets but tiny ice crystals. They often appear with wind and mean the weather is going to change. These wispy clouds (right) are cirrus clouds.

How cloudy is it?

The amount of cloud cover is measured by working out how much of the sky is actually covered by clouds. This can be shown by drawing a circle and partly shading it.

No clouds in sky.

A few clouds present.

Half the sky is covered with clouds.

Clouds cover most of the sky.

The sky is completely covered with clouds.

This method makes it easy to write down how much cloud cover is present. Look outside now. How much cloud cover is there? What symbol would you draw?

RAIN, SNOW AND HAIL

Water is always being moved around in a cycle. Water **evaporates** from the land and sea and turns into water vapour. The water vapour forms clouds. The water in the clouds is returned to the land as rain, snow or hail. This water finds its way into rivers and streams and finally back to the sea.

This water cycle has been going on for millions of years. The rain you see falling today has fallen millions of times before and will continue to do so.

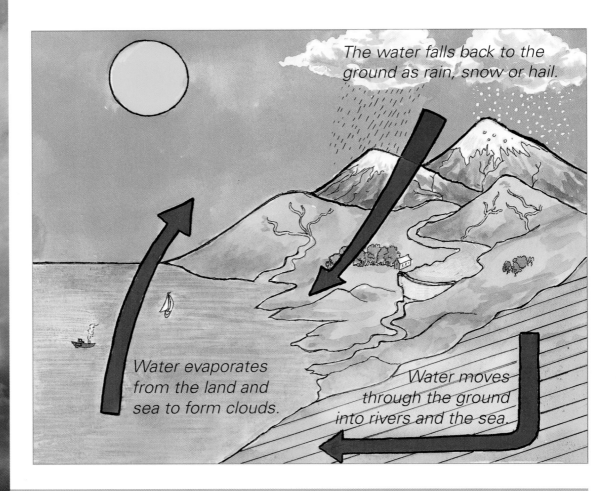

The water falls back to the ground as rain, snow or hail.

Water evaporates from the land and sea to form clouds.

Water moves through the ground into rivers and the sea.

WHAT MAKES IT RAIN?

The tiny water droplets inside clouds are constantly moving around. They bump into each other, join together and slowly get bigger and bigger. When they get heavy, they start to fall, picking up smaller droplets on the way. Finally they fall out of the cloud as raindrops. We measure the amount of rain that has fallen using a rain gauge.

PROJECT

Make a rain gauge.

You will need:
a clear plastic bottle
scissors
a ruler
some waterproof tape
a waterproof pen.

1. Get an adult to help you cut the top off the bottle.

2. Using the ruler as a guide, draw a centimetre scale on the water-proof tape and stick it on the side of the bottle.

3. Fit the top of the bottle, turned upside down, into the base of the bottle as a funnel.

4. Put the rain gauge in an open area in your garden. (You may need to support it with some stones to keep it from falling over.)

5. Record the rainfall once a day. If there is not enough rain to measure properly, you can write down 'trace'. Don't forget to empty the gauge after you have measured the rain each day.

SNOW

When it is very cold, the water droplets in clouds freeze into snow crystals. These crystals join together to make snowflakes. Snowflakes are always six-sided, but no two are ever the same.

If the **temperature** remains below freezing, they will reach the ground as snow. Often, though, they will meet warmer air and melt, turning into rain.

A coal train travels through a snowstorm.

The morning after a heavy snowfall.

HAIL

Hail only forms inside huge storm clouds. Tiny pieces of ice are blown around inside the cloud. They gradually get bigger as they collect more layers of ice on the way. When they get quite heavy, they fall out of the cloud as hailstones. If you ask an adult to cut a hailstone open, you will see the layers of ice that have built up inside it.

Hailstones in the grass.

RAINBOWS

Rainbows appear when it is raining and the Sun is shining at the same time. Sunlight is actually made up of six colours: red, orange, yellow, green, blue and violet. When a ray of sunlight enters a raindrop, it is split up into all these colours, and these are what we see from the ground. You must have your back to the Sun to see a rainbow.

Rainbows actually form a complete circle. Because Earth is in the way, you can only ever see half a circle from the ground.

Sometimes you can see the whole circular rainbow from an aeroplane.

An autumn rainbow.

DEW, MIST, FOG AND FROST

Dew, mist, fog and frost are also formed from water vapour in the air. Dew forms on cold, clear nights when water droplets **condense** on to cold surfaces such as grass, plants or cobwebs. The dew **evaporates** when the Sun comes out during the day. If the **temperature** of the air falls below freezing, the dew turns to ice crystals and covers everything with frost.

▲ *Early morning dew on spiders' webs.*

Mist and fog are actually clouds that form near the ground. Like other clouds they are made when the air is full of water vapour. If the distance you can see is less than 1 kilometre (0.6 miles), the cloud is called fog. Otherwise the air filled with moisture is called mist.

Driving in fog can be very dangerous.

THUNDERSTORMS

Sometimes cumulus clouds grow into huge, tall cumulonimbus clouds. These clouds often bring thunderstorms. **Static electricity** that builds up in the clouds is released as a huge spark. This is what we see as lightning. As it passes, the lightning heats the air which expands very quickly and causes the crashing sound of thunder.

Because light travels faster than sound, you see the lightning before you hear the thunder. If you start counting when you see the lightning, you can work out roughly how far away the storm is. For every 5 seconds you count, the storm is 1.6 kilometres (1 mile) away.

HURRICANES

Sometimes when warm air rises over tropical oceans, it forms a very violent storm. In the USA and the Caribbean these storms are called **hurricanes**. They are also called typhoons, cyclones or willy-willies in other parts of the world. Hurricanes bring very strong winds of up to 300 kilometres (185 miles) per hour.

Hurricanes rip up trees, destroy crops and ruin buildings, sometimes flattening whole towns.

TORNADOES

The very worst storms of all are called tornadoes. Tornadoes are small, extremely powerful whirlwinds that form under

thunderclouds. The wind speed inside them can reach 500 kilometres (300 miles) per hour. No one is sure exactly how fast it is, because none of the instruments used to record wind speed has ever survived a really strong tornado!

Tornadoes are most common in the Midwest of the USA where about 500 occur every year.

WEATHER FORECASTS

A **prediction** of the weather is called a weather forecast. To some people, weather forecasts are very important. Farmers need to know what the weather is doing, so they know the best times to sow, spray and harvest their crops. Airports need to know when snow, fog or ice are expected, so they can decide whether to close the runways. Fishermen and other sailors rely on weather forecasts to tell them about the winds and weather they can expect at sea.

An impressive storm cloud builds up at the coast in East Sussex, England.

COLLECTING INFORMATION

In order to make weather forecasts, scientists called **meteorologists** collect information from all around the world. This information is sent in from thousands of weather stations on land, ships and in aircraft. Weather **satellites** in space send down pictures of cloud formations.

All this information is fed into computers and studied by the meteorologists. Then they can make a picture of what is happening in the **atmosphere** and what weather can be expected in the next few days.

*This satellite picture shows a **hurricane** developing off the coast of Mexico.*

PROJECT

Be a weather recorder!

If you have carried out all the projects in this book, you will have enough equipment to make your own personal weather station. Using a small notebook, try recording the weather for a week.

Don't forget to measure:
- the amount of rain each day
- the amount and type of cloud cover
- the temperature at the same time each day
- the direction of the wind
- the number of hours of sunshine each day.

Monday
Rain 1cm
cloud ☁3◑
Temp 21°C
Wind NW

Tuesday

CLIMATE

Climate is the pattern of weather a place receives over a long period of time. The climate of any area depends on its position on Earth's surface. Countries near the **equator** have a hot climate because they receive more sunshine. Both the Poles have very cold climates.

Climate also depends on how near to the sea a place is and how high it is.

A tropical rainforest in Costa Rica. Tropical rainforests grow in regions near the equator between the tropics of Cancer and Capricorn. They are warm all year round and have a high rainfall with rain falling nearly every day. Tropical rainforests are home to over half the animal and plant **species** in the world.

A temperate woodland in Europe. Conifers and broadleaved trees grow in temperate forests. These forests are found in parts of Europe and North America. Temperate regions have distinct **seasons** with cold winters and warm summers.

tropic of Cancer

equator

tropic of Capricorn

A desert in Egypt, Africa. Deserts are the driest places on Earth. Most have less than 10 centimetres of rain in a year. Some have no rain for many years at a time. Most deserts are hot, so it is difficult for plants to grow. Without plants, animals and people find it hard to live, too.

GLOSSARY

anemometer instrument for measuring wind speed in kilometres or miles per hour

atmosphere layer of gases surrounding Earth

condensation process when water vapour cools and turns to water

equator imaginary line around the centre of Earth

evaporation process when a liquid, like water, turns into a gas

hurricane very powerful, swirling storm

meteorologist scientist who studies the weather and the atmosphere

predict to work out what is going to happen

satellite unmanned spacecraft orbiting Earth or another planet to gather information

season particular time of year that has certain weather conditions. Spring, summer, autumn and winter are all seasons.

species type or kind of animal or plant

static electricity electrical charge held by an object

temperature how hot or cold something is

thermometer instrument used to measure temperature

FURTHER INFORMATION

BOOKS

Climate Crisis, Nigel Hawkes (Franklin Watts, 2003)

Disasters in Nature: Hurricanes, Catherine Chambers (Heinemann Library, 2000)

DK Guide to Weather, Michael Allaby (Dorling Kindersley, 2000)

Measuring the Weather: Sunshine and Clouds, Angella Streluk and Alan Rodgers (Heinemann Library, 2002)

Nature on the Rampage: Tornadoes, Jim Steele (Raintree, 2003)

Weather, Chris Oxlade (Hodder Wayland, 2001)

WEBSITES

Met Office – take a look at the world's weather news and click on 'Learn about the weather' for information and activities on all aspects of weather from rainbows to the seasons.
http://www.metoffice.com

What is weather? – learn about the weather, from wind direction to sunshine, and how this affects people all over the world.
http://www.bbc.co.uk/schools/whatisweather

World weather – find out the latest weather forecasts for where you live, and for different countries all around the world.
http://www.bbc.co.uk/weather

Disclaimer
All the Internet addresses (URLs) given in this book were valid at the time of going to press. However, due to the dynamic nature of the Internet, some addresses may have changed, or sites may have ceased to exist since publication. While the author and publishers regret any inconvenience this may cause readers, no responsibility for any such changes can be accepted by either the author or the publishers.

INDEX

air 10, 11
anemometer 12
atmosphere 8, 11, 27

Beaufort scale 12

cirrus clouds 17
climate 28, 29
clouds 6, 14, 15, 18, 23, 26
condensation 14, 15
cumulonimbus clouds 24
cumulus clouds 16, 24
cyclone 25

dew 23

Earth 8, 11, 28
electricity 24
equator 8, 28
evaporation 14, 15, 18

farmers 26
fishermen 26
fog 23
frost 23

hail 18, 21
hurricane 12, 13, 25, 27

ice 14, 17

lightning 24

meteorologists 26, 27
mist 23

North Pole 8

rain 6, 18
rain gauge 19
rainbow 22

satellite 26
seasons 27
snow 6, 18, 20, 21
South Pole 8
stratus clouds 16
summer 6
Sun 8, 11, 22
sunshine 6

temperature 9
thermometer 9
thunder 24
thunderstorms 6, 24
tornado 25
trade winds 11
typhoon 25

water cycle 18
water vapour 14, 18
weather forecast 7, 26, 27
weather vane 12, 13
willy-willy 25
wind 6, 10, 17
winter 6